THE
SACRED HEART
OF TREES

TONI CARMINE SALERNO

BLUE ANGEL®
PUBLISHING

The Sacred Heart of Trees

Published by Blue Angel Publishing
80 Glen Tower Drive, Glen Waverley,
Victoria, Australia 3150
E-mail: info@blueangelonline.com
Website: www.blueangelonline.com

Text by Toni Carmine Salerno, except where noted.
Artwork by Toni Carmine Salerno
Edited by Tanya Graham

Blue Angel is a registered trademark of Blue Angel Gallery Pty. Ltd.

ISBN: 978-1-922161-40-6

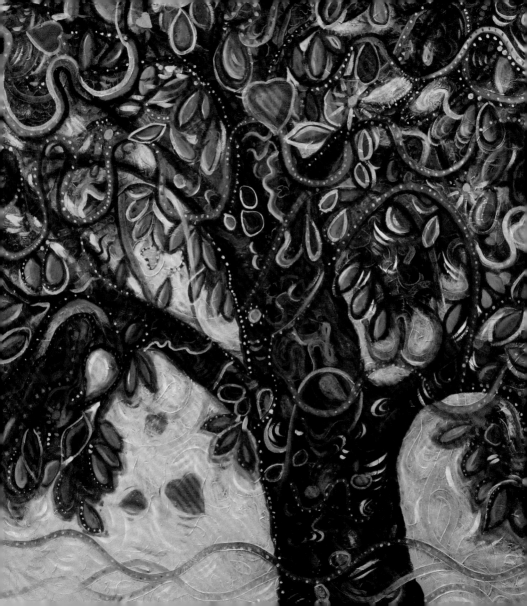

Introduction

I have always loved trees and from a very early age I have felt a deep spiritual connection with them. I find them so amazingly beautiful, soulful and full of character. To me they are alive, they breathe, they are wise and loving. I am always inspired and moved by them. And my love and fascination for trees grows deeper as I get older. No matter where I am in the world I always find solace and comfort in trees. They are like old friends. I love touching and connecting with them. I feel blessed and loved by them and I never tire of painting them.

They have been a major theme in my work from when I first began painting. As you will see in a lot of my work, my trees are often part tree and part human, or they have wings and hearts. I suppose this is my way of saying that each tree has a soul and spirit. I hope that this little book may inspire you to look at trees differently and perhaps see and feel them the way I do.

You can use this book as an oracle, opening it randomly at any page for a message, or you can read through it in the usual way, from cover to cover, if you prefer. Perhaps it will help you see and feel life from a more spiritual perspective, and strengthen your connection to your own spiritual and creative nature, which is unlimited and transcends both time and space.

One of my guiding principles is that everything is essentially energy; an intelligent creative energy which connects us all spiritually. That energy is an inner light that exists within me and you and every blade of grass. It is in the air, the trees, the oceans and streams. It is within sunlight, in the stars, earth and sky; and even exists within darkness.

The writings in this book are my own unless otherwise stated. I have included a few quotes from some of my favourite people.

My writings are mainly poetic and don't really need to be understood by the mind. Hopefully, along with the images, they will flow into your heart. That is all that is needed. They do not need to be understood, because just like our 'inner light', they are ultimately beyond words and description.

With love and eternal blessings,
Toni Carmine Salerno

Look within
you will find something beautiful
something sacred
something sweet
something more than my words
can describe to you

Feel it all around you,
feel it inside

The all-embracing
creative force of life

Love fills everything
with the same love,
the same divine force,
that moves the earth,
stars and universe.
It fills the trees, the earth
and each blade of grass,
it flows through ocean waves,
through the sky and air.
It forever expands
in my heart and soul,
in your heart and soul.

Spirit is the heart of matter;
matter is the ensoulment of spirit.

– Gaston Bachelard

My fear dissolves when I feel
the all-embracing creative force of love
flowing through me, flowing through you
and all of life upon this planet.
Love is a universe inside you,
it is this beautiful, tender
and at times painful dream called life.

Love knows all there is to know about us
But she does not know what we shall become
Or to what heights we may ascend
Or the universes we may give birth to
For some things cannot be known, not even to her

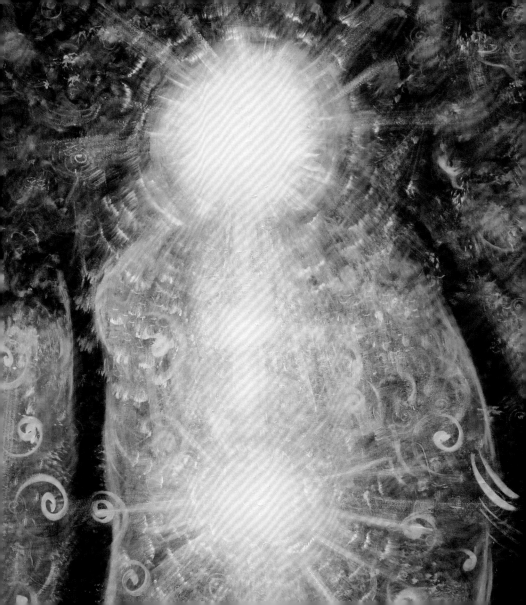

Beyond the noise of this world,
there is a point of stillness, of peace and silence.
Within you there is a point of infinite peace, love and joy.
Within you there is a sacred place where love is always present,
where love is always waiting patiently for you to return.
There is no better time than now for you to return,
there is no time but now to go within,
to discover the infinite world of love, peace and joy
that is the true you.

When the deep meaning of things is not understood
the mind's essential peace is disturbed to no avail.
The way is perfect like vast space
where nothing is lacking and nothing is in excess.
Indeed, it is due to our choosing to accept or reject
that we do not see the true nature of things.

– *Sosan*

This breath, this moment, this dream
that floats through my mind...
All appears, disappears, is born, dies and is born again,
transformed, transfigured by love....
Glowing mother, my seed of dreams,
dark mother, goddess,
nourishing, nurturing, giver of life and destroyer...

Look at the trees, look at the birds,
look at the clouds, look at the stars...
and if you have eyes you will be able to see
that the whole existence is joyful.
Everything is simply happy.
Trees are happy for no reason;
they are not going to become prime ministers or presidents
and they are not going to become rich
and they will never have any bank balance.
Look at the flowers – for no reason.
It is simply unbelievable how happy flowers are.

– Osho

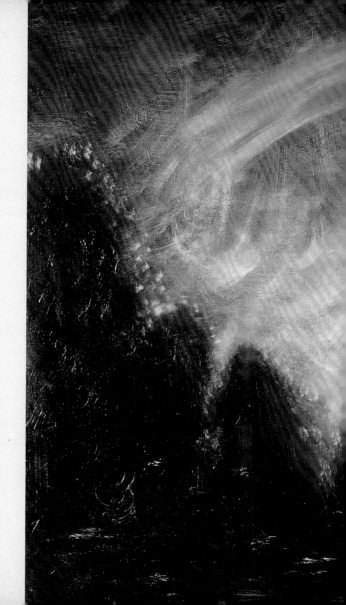

Through a
silent whisper,
or a gentle breeze,
through looking at
the stars at night,
through a thought
or feeling,
or the spirit of trees
or a leaf of grass
Through a
ray of light,
a word or smile,
you can feel
the presence of love.

Beyond this mind,
that in this moment is thinking
about what to say or how to say it,
there is a higher mind,
that says everything
without thinking or speaking.

upon a time in a dream, I
...nt of you, I was standing
the bank and you appeared
upon a time in a dream, I
...ember the wind blew through
I remember the sky opened
and heaven appeared, shining
...ugh the raindrops like a crys...
...dom of divine light. Through
...ages I dreamt, I continued to
...am of you and sometimes
...came to me, you entered
...ened up your heart and
...ped in. Once upon a time
...dream I remember se...
for the very first
...once wa...

Once upon a time, here on Earth,
...in the bank and my roots penetrat...
...earth and the rain fell and the
...lid su... and the... world did te...
and the birds sang and other trees g...
...up around me, but still, I felt lo...
...because I missed you and somet...
...you came to me in my dreams...
...the world continued to turn and
...told you that I loved you and you
...told me that you loved me and
...the world turned and the moon
...and the days unfolded their...to
...of all that has come and gone...
...ll that shall come and go, of s...
...ows and light and rainbows a...
...still I continued to dream of you
...sometimes you came to me an...
...held me in my dreams and th...
...sky opened up and heaven...
...appeared and cry...

In the silence of nature
the poetry of the earth can be heard.
In the stillness of your heart
the poetry of your divine self.
An unspoken word may contain a thousand prayers,
whilst the heart of every tree is filled with infinite joy.
A ray of sunshine flows through the trees,
the wind blows and a leaf falls to the ground
and the earth smiles
and there is peace.

Eternity
is a
very long
time
yet it is
also
no time
at all

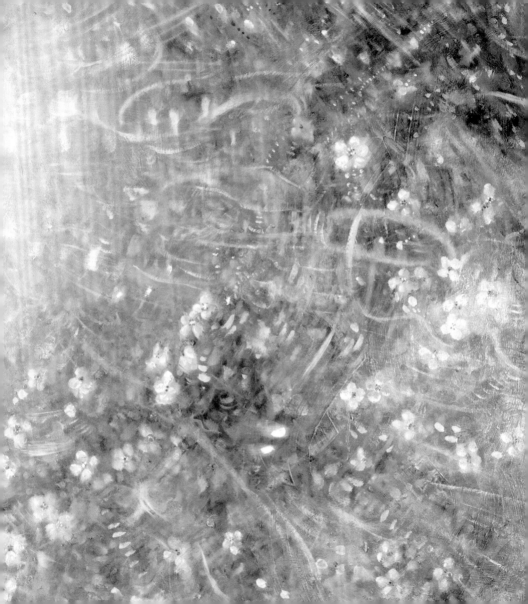

Walking through a beautiful forest,
all the thoughts of the world leave and my mind is clear
like an infinite blue sky.
I am present and feel the presence of a beautiful gentle soul.
It is a great and powerful presence as well,
like a great light glowing beside me, around me, inside me.
I look at the trees, I can see inside their hearts.
There is a small flame glowing inside each one.
There is an aura of love, a soul,
many beautiful souls within this forest of trees.
I feel the embrace of the Divine Mother, Gaia, Goddess,
her spirit flowing through my heart
like a mighty river flowing through the earth.
She flows through all our hearts,
through our thoughts and dreams.
Indeed, she is the dreamer inside us,
inviting us to enter her infinite and eternal ocean of love.

O time, O space, O spaceless and timeless soul,
within and beyond this dream of earth and sky,
where past, future and now are always present.
O forgotten soul, I have not forgotten you,
nor the seamless thread of life and passing.
I embrace you now,
no matter where in life or death you are,
with the spirit of these words.

But let there be spaces in your togetherness
and let the winds of the heavens dance between you.
Love one another but make not a bond of love:
let it rather be a moving sea between the shores of your souls.

– Khalil Gibran

Dear Mother Earth,
thank you for all your love,
thank you for this beautiful dream of life
that you weave inside my heart,
Thank you for your embrace
and enfolding petals of love.

In a dream I saw the Divine Mother
but it is hard to describe her appearance
for she seems to embody the beauty of the entire world
and personify the wisdom of every age and culture.
Before her shimmering changing form
I was drawn to a point of light glowing from her mind and heart.
I entered a vast space with no beginning or end,
where my soul, by her grace,
was endlessly transforming to ever-greater love.

Every atom of you is love
Every part of your beautiful soul is love
Every thought of you is love

Life is an ocean of dreams that contains the entire universe,
and deeper still an endless number of universes.
Life is a particle of light that contains every other particle,
and deeper still, the dark void from which all light is born,
and deeper still, the absolute which contains no life
but every possibility.

The trees smile as I walk by, they embrace me spiritually within their leaves and branches and love me. My spirit reaches out to them and I embrace them lovingly in return. The sky blesses me with rain and I feel nourished. My soul reaches up and merges with its infinite expanse. I love the sky and rain. A ray of sunlight flows into my heart and a great healing light fills my mind and thoughts – a part of me remembers that I once was the sun.

I send rays of loving thoughts back to the sun and thank the sun for giving me life. I feel the earth beneath my feet and know that I am supported by the great blessed mother. I place my hand upon her skin and sense the pounding beat of her heart, ocean waves and flowing rivers, I sense her molten fiery core and my love flows out to her and I know that from within the heart of this earth many future earths shall be born.

I keep on walking and a flower opens its petals as if to greet me. A little bird tweets hello and time stands still for a moment and all I feel is love.

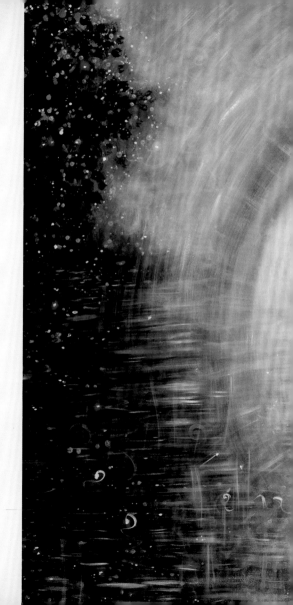

Beyond the crashing
waves of thought
there is a tranquil ocean
where my soul floats
towards the great glowing sun,
and looking around me
in this peaceful state,
I dream that I am an infinite sky.
A gentle breeze blows
and flowers float
through the air,
and I realise that all this is me.
I am the crashing
waves of thought,
I am the tranquil ocean,
I am the dream,
the breeze, the flowers,
the infinite sky.

A wound
is the place
where light
enters you.

– Rumi

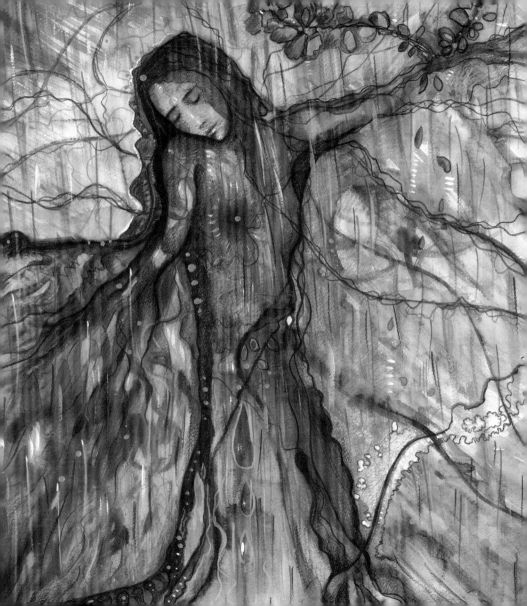

I whisper to the air
and she responds with a gentle breeze

I touch a tree
and a leaf falls to reminds me that I'm loved

I think about this beautiful planet,
a ray of sunlight fills me with hope

I gaze at the night sky
and a galaxy of stars illuminates my heart

Nowhere can man find
a quieter or more untroubled retreat
than in his own soul.

– Marcus Aurelius (121-180 CE)

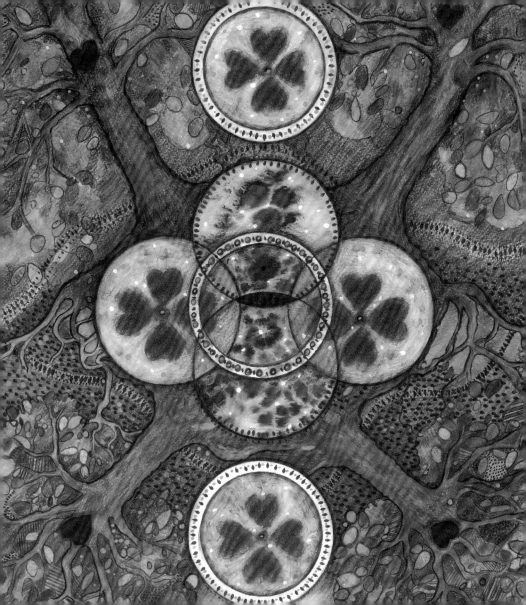

Often I have come to you
Often I have smiled at you
Often I have carried you
Always I will love you

The Divine Mother is kundalini sleeping within us,
without worshipping Her we can never know ourselves.
All-merciful, all-powerful, omnipresent are attributes
of the Divine Mother. She is the sum total of the energy
of the universe. Every manifestation of power in the universe is
'Mother.' She is life. She is intelligence. She is love.
She is the universe, yet separate from it.

– Swami Vivekananda, 1st June 1895

Today I will love and accept
both the positive and negative aspects of myself and others.
Today I will love and accept myself as I am
and accept the world as it is.
Today I remember that everything out there
is also inside me.

in the land of
my dreams, I
you and you
an angel from
the earth beneath
feet, like a dream
in a dream, a
in a flower, a
in a world. you
me to me and
heart and
life with
In the beginning the wind
into our hearts and the
wind did howl and our
were united by the love that
moved the wind and by
force that created love
one day the wind slowed
night down and the sky
still and blue and
seasons changed and the
leaves changed colour
my soul expanded and
I embraced the
and loved you

When the mind
is not at war
with the heart,
there is peace.

The
empty
space
between
each
thought
is a
gateway
to infinite
peace.

A million years have passed
and still the same light glows in my heart
and the same love fills my soul.

The universe is inside you
and within that universe
is an infinite number of other universes

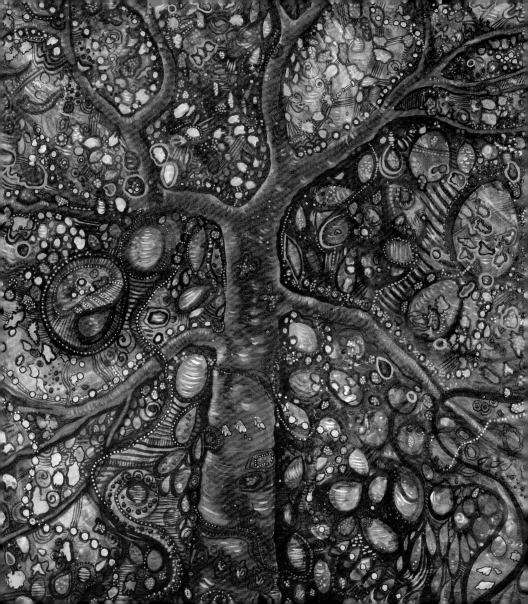

Something
within you
contains the
uncontainable,
untamed you

This time will never come again
but it will never cease either.

When I was a little girl, there was nothing quite so magical to me as trees. Stepping amongst their trunks, slipping out of the hot summer sun into cool relief underneath their branches. Such peace. I was free, happy and loved. I felt purity in their presence. Yes, their presence. I was amongst friends, you see.

I always knew them as living, sentient beings. When I felt a breeze rustling their leaves, it was as though they were slipping their finger-like branches through my hair. I was often distraught by life experiences, being such a sensitive child, and I would unconsciously seek them out. What else could provide such unconditional and instant relief? Their soothing, healing peace restored my soul. Though, the love I felt for them could also overwhelm me. Seeing trees felled on television distressed me so deeply. I would cry in genuine grief. My heart is the lover of this perennial beloved. A love affair that began in childhood and I am yet to grow out of. I suspect I never will.

– Alana Fairchild

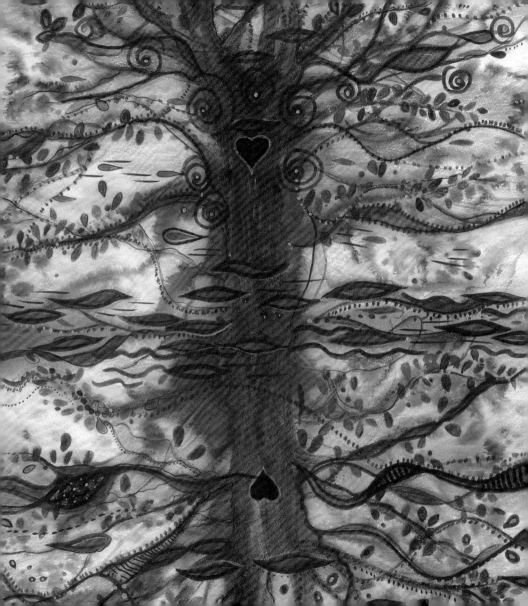

On a grassy hill
a majestic oak tree gazes at the night sky.
Leaves caressed by a gentle breeze,
he reflects on life and its changing seasons.
He remembers....
the summer rain,
autumn's golden light
and falling leaves,
winter's grey clouds
and spring's crystal clarity and blossoming.
On a grassy hill one night
a beautiful oak reflects on his life
and sheds a tear of joy.

Before I came on this earth, Father, I was the same.
As a little girl, I was the same.
I grew into womanhood, but still I was the same....
Ever afterwards though the dance of creation changes around me
in the hall of eternity, I shall be the same.

– Anandamayi Ma

There are only two ways to live your life.
One is as though nothing is a miracle.
The other is as though everything is a miracle.

– Albert Einstein

The smallest thing
can have infinite potential

The power of the entire universe
is present even in a leaf of grass

You will never have any more than you have now
...because you have everything now.

Life is always moving and circumstances always changing.
Nothing is ever settled. Just when you think things are,
something happens that unsettles you. A river of thoughts flows
through your mind and a sea of emotion ebbs and flows in your
heart. One moment you are happy, one moment you are sad.
One moment there is peace and in the next moment there is war.
This is what it is to be human, you can't escape it.
And yet, just beyond the surface of all this human drama,
a whole other world exists, one of infinite love, wisdom and joy.
It is a world called soul, and whether you know it or not, or agree
to it or not, you have one. Soul is the real you, the eternal you, it is
your truth, your peace, infinitely wise, loving and compassionate.
This is what it is to be spiritual and you can't escape it.
So give thanks for all that you are, and for all that is seen or
unseen. Be equally grateful for your physical and spiritual realities
for ultimately your earthly experiences are simply a dream. What
is real is the infinite light of your soul. Remember who you are.
In physical form you are an actor playing out a role on the world
stage while spiritually you are both director and author.

I bequeath myself to the dirt to grow from the grass I love,
If you want me again look for me under your boot-soles.
You will hardly know who I am or what I mean,
But I shall be good health to you nevertheless,
and filter and fibre your blood.
Failing to fetch me at first keep encouraged,
missing me one place search another,
I stop somewhere waiting for you.

– Walt Whitman

Millions of years from now...
the earth has transformed to light,
we and every species that ever existed
on physical earth are here,
luminous in our new light bodies,
able to travel faster than light.
We see new colours
through previously hidden dimensions,
we see the angels,
talk to them and touch them,
we welcome change
because we know it is
the driving force of life.
We see the soul and spirit of everything.
Millions of years from now
our story continues...

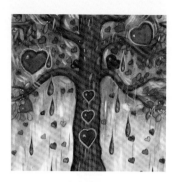

Looking for God
From gathered Sufi Wisdom

There was a man who wanted to find God. He took his backpack, filled it with what he felt he needed for a long journey of pilgrimage, said goodbye to friends and relatives and left his home and town in search of God. He told everyone that he would return when his backpack was filled with God.

On the way, a few miles away from his home, he noticed a small seedling that had grown next to the road. He gazed at the seedling, and said aloud, "How sad to be next to the road and not able to move."

The seedling heard the traveler and said, "The real pain is to spend a long time in search of something and never be able to find it."

The traveler laughed at the seedling and said, "What do you know about search? You are stuck in the mud and unable to experience the joy of searching for something." He moved on and did not hear the seedling saying, "What you are looking for is right here!"

The traveler continued his journey to search for God. Weeks, months, years and decades passed, but he was unable to find God. He used up all the supplies he had in his backpack and was unable to find a single sign or clue to help him find God. Exhausted and disappointed, he decided to return home.

When the traveler was within a few miles of his town, he noticed a tall beautiful tree next to the road. Its branches were heavily laden with fruit and flowering blossoms, and were covered with green leaves. He picked some of the fruit from the tree and sat in the shade beneath the branches, leaning against the trunk of the tree. He did not recognize the tree as the small seedling he had seen when he left, but the tree recognized and remembered the traveler.

"Hello traveler, what do you have in your backpack?" the tree asked the traveler. "Would you care to share some with me?"

"I am ashamed to tell you that my backpack is empty," said the traveler.

The tree said to him, "Now that your backpack is empty, you have everything. Many years ago you passed by here, when I was only a small unimportant seedling, and your backpack was full of everything, including your ego thinking you could find God somewhere out there. Now that you have lost everything, you are ready to truly be able to receive God." The tree poured the secrets of a greater Truth into the man's backpack.

Suddenly, the traveler became aware that the Presence of God was with him. Surprised with what he was feeling and experiencing, he said to the tree, "I traveled from town to town for decades and could not find God. How were you able to discover God without taking a step out of this mud?"

The tree said, "You were looking for God outside of your own self, and you kept losing all the riches you had! I searched for God inside of me, and every moment of every day became richer, more powerful, more beautiful, and more fruitful than ever before. You did not search within you, for it seemed to be much easier for you to look outside and beyond your own being than it was to awaken to the presence of God within your own self."

– Rassouli

About the Artist & Author

My art is beyond words, it requires no thinking. There is nothing to understand, they are just colours, feelings and emotions that are felt in the heart. An open heart is all that is required. There is no particular meaning, each work may trigger something in the viewer or it may not. Each work is simply about love.

Toni Carmine Salerno is the author of many books, meditation recordings and oracle cards. He is also an artist who paints intuitively, creating works that are infused with a timeless sense of love. Born in Melbourne, Australia to Italian parents, the work of this internationally acclaimed self-taught artist and author and his publishing house, Blue Angel Publishing, continues to have a significant and positive effect on people's lives around the globe, connecting people and cultures through the universal language of love.

You can find out more by visiting **www.tonicarminesalerno.com** or **www.blueangelonline.com**

For more information on this
or any Blue Angel Publishing release,
please visit our website at:

www.blueangelonline.com